The Ni▮ Before OFSTED Came

and other poems by
Tony Rowlands
drawings by Tammy Copp

ISBN 978-0-9559210-0-1

Published by ArBeth Media
31, Glena Avenue, Knowle, Bristol BS4 2LB.

Printed by Doveton Press, Bristol.

Contents

THE NIGHT BEFORE OFSTED CAME
A True Story

The night before OFSTED came, I had a dream.
I was teaching, in one of those sheds which crowd like wrecks
Round the breeze-block cliffs of schools,
A year 8 group, sharp with hope.
Their faces flicked from mine, to the door,
And I turned, to see four sets of bleached eyes
Above black suits, filched from a horror movie.
THEM. Gulp.

I cowered back to the class, and the dream
Accelerated. The walls of the room cracked apart,
The ceiling softly exploded, and the floor fell away,
Into a savage sea.
Desks slid into the surf, launching silent, screaming kids.
I hurled myself at the flailing emergency,
And shoved the bodies back, up the wooden beach
Towards the creepy four.

"How'm I doing?" I shouted, armpit deep, a kid in each fist.
The response echoed out of the Film Noir lighting:
"We think you read the funeral oration with some style."

WOW. I drove to work,
Numb in the knowledge
That Boris Karloff was just behind,
In a black sedan, and also, that I had
AN APPOINTMENT.

She was late. A lady from a John Major bicycling memoir,
Snug and beaming. "I'm having such a lovely time," she said.
I needed to hold on to something. "That's nice," I said,
But she hadn't got time to chat.
She'd got a life, and she needed a witness, someone to be impressed.
There was the hotel for a start, agreeably expensive, leafily located,
The private jollity of pre-dinner gin, menus in French, and hairdressing
On the house.

And then there was all that money,
(The kids were listening now)
And cups of tea and coffee from a pot.

I wanted Boris back. I needed a swim.
"How'm doing?" I said. Straight out. I'd had enough.
She looked them over. How is it, d'you think,
That kids can find such pleasure
In pretending to be innocent? (Oh, I will pay. Believe me, I will pay.)
She turned back to me, her eyes damp with nostalgia.
"Marvellous," she said, "absolutely marvellous." Well, I deserved it.
I saved them from drowning, didn't I?

On my way out of school, later that day,
I saw her again, through an open door,
Snoring happily in a department meeting
That she was supposed to be observing.
I stopped, and smiled at the pale faces attached to the table.
"D'you think we should wake her up?" someone said.
"No," I said, "let her dream."

BEING WATCHED

The brains behind Big Brother
Sometimes dreams
That he has been imprisoned
Inside his own creation.

Neighbours scramble for their mobiles
When his screams
Become insistent,
Above the scented quiet

Of their moonlit, sought-after village.
Although what seems
At first glance
An enviable location, drenched in electronic safety,

Where restored smithy and ostler's cottage,
Whose unearthed beams
And honeysuckled porch
Recall those sunlit meadow days

When wood smoke curled from chimney pots
And ice creams
Bought at summer fetes,
Lasted all the way

To evening harvest home,
And streams
Of blazered children
Chattered to games on the piggyback green,

Has yet about its lanes a wreath of drifting unease,
As if, in secret, gleams
A shadowed eye, watching every scripted movement,
And judging every freshly painted hope.

A WAR BY CANDLELIGHT

The glass slewed.
I caught all but a few drops.
"No problem," the waiter said,
But we knew your jabbing fingers,
Fencing across the table,
Cut through more than etiquette.
You stood, stepped out of the arena,
And smiled, as Franco
Helped you with your coat.
"Arriverderci, Signora."
A tilt of the head for
The countless games
He'd counted out.
You walked left, past Kettners,
Out of sight, to Cambridge Circus.
As I contemplated the ashes
Of a war by candlelight,
Franco curved towards me,
The bill held primly to his heart.
"Everything to your satisfaction,
Signore?"

X Factor.

As night began, the funeral ceremonies were still in progress,
And would continue well into the next day,
A circumstance which disturbed the management of the facility,
Who were, by and large, opposed to precedents.
But so many crowded the reception hall,
Hoping to go through to the second stage.

At their tables, the judges briskly reminded the entrants
That their requests should conform in every detail,
And that the wailing of old songs should not reveal
The slightest deviation from the accepted mode of presentation.
Only by sticking to the rules, the judges indicated,
Could the hopeful proceed to the second stage.

Relatives, and particularly mothers who cried easily, and who
Agreed to be costumed by the organisers in a way which might
Appeal to an audience on a Caribbean cruise holiday,
Were carefully posed on the scaffold surrounding the event.

The entrants, one by one, submitted their wailing to scrutiny,
While cameras swooped from gantries, and the orchestra sighed,
And the seated judges exchanged professional glances,
Or nodded their heads importantly.

Those rejected were sent back, often with words of brutal finality,
Less often with an invitation to have another go, at a later date.
The chosen ones, still vibrating with the energy of their action,
Stared across the shining floor, at family members and friends,
Who had given such generous support, in preparing for the trial,
And who would now witness the movement to the second stage.

Thoughts in a School Corridor

In the tunnel the faces
Drain,
Under the wall the orchids
Strain
To the sounds of fear.

Yet over the green, young Angels
Beguile,
Stretch and renew the human
Style,
For the coming year.

CHOKEY

An unusual cat. Sister of Cheesey.

The truth is, we took it for granted,
That somehow you'd always be here,
Your enquiring eyes at the window,
On the floor with your feet in the air.

You allowed us to share in your story,
You claimed private places to snooze,
You determinedly dribbled on jumpers,
You warmed winter duvets with Cheese.

And now, though the house seems so empty,
We know you'll make light of the years,
Asleep in the crook of the arm of the night,
With your paws on a pillow of stars.

A MARITIME ADVENTURE
On Baltic Wharf, Bristol.

I thought I was on the starboard tack
When the Commodore shouted "Water!"
Then I saw the gleam in those sailor's eyes,
And knew he'd give no quarter.

He whacked my gaff with a sickening crack,
And both of us went down,
And I heard my old man's sound advice,
"Wear some cork, or drown."

The wind was gusting five that day,
From out of Underfall Yard,
And brave men reefed the mainsail,
And pulled the sheets in hard.

In the howling foam of that dockland gale
I thought I was bound for glory,
'Til I heard the sound that sailors cheer,
T'was Keith in his little dory.

With soothing words, and nautical skill
He brought me back from the brink,
And towing behind him along to the wharf,
Gave me the time to think

That I love this little patch of surf,
And the week end sailing day,
But next time I launch, I'll remember the rule
"Keep out of the Commodore's way!"

I Knew You

I loved you before you were born,
And I will love you
Long after you take your place
Back among the stars.

We belong to the same errant tribe,
You and me.
We have wandered the universe
For all the time that there was,
Looking for firm ground.

We met in this room,
As if by design,
And recognised, without speaking,
The other's membership.

And Then There Was ENRON.

And then we found
That ENRON
Had our politicians
By the throat,
And that those public spirits
Lacked the taste
For facing down the dismal authority
Of someone else's money.
Were we outraged?
If the gentlemen callers
Had been gently acquainted
With the duties of office,
And promises made
At election time,
And marched in chains
And balaclavas
To the nearest seaport,
Then we might have allowed ourselves
A momentary glimpse
Into a moderately dignified future.
As it is, each press conference
Confirmed our ticket to the bleak cabaret
Of broken pledges mixed with spin,
And the passing interest lay
In contemplating
How those owners of probity
Would emerge from the trough
With reputations untarnished.

A PEERAGE FOR SALE

A Peerage? Of course, sir.
Let me take your measurements.
Bank statement?
Ooh, aren't we a big boy.
Off shore accounts?
Just hold the tape there,
Would you, sir?
Mmm. You do stand out from the crowd.
And just pass your hand over that
If you'd be so kind.
Genuine Ermine, sir.
Very "in" this year.
As I've no doubt you know.

Resting Luvvie. Winter 1967.

On the dole
Heart and soul
Are torn apart.
An endless chart
Of shattered days
Amaze, amaze
The thwarted mind
And body. Be kind!
I roar to fate
But the golden gate
Stays shut. Oh Hell!
Switch on Big L,
And stare, stare
At the trees, now bare,
Shiftless too
Like you, and you,
Comma in time,
A fruitless mime
Of love and hate,
Wait! Wait! Wait!
Stopping is dying
I think, sighing
In my chair,
Grey is my hair,
Or white. Jerk!
Get back to work!

THE BALLAD OF NED LUDD

Ned Ludd he was a working man,
He rose to greet the dawn,
He weaved his cloth,
And he sowed his seed,
And he scythed his own dear corn.

T'was freedoms road he walked upon,
No gate stood in his way;
He smiled at fate
And his children ate,
'Til Progress had its day.

'Til Progress had its day, my dear,
'Til Progress had its day.

The Bailiff said "There's laws been made,
By men in London town,
To take your land,
And smash your loom,
And tear your cottage down."

"For industry must mint its coin,
To build a rich man's hall,
Bills must be met
From a poor man's sweat,
When Progress comes to call."

"When Progress comes to call, my boy,
When Progress comes to call."

Brave Ned then cried "I scorn your laws!
And will my cudgel wield!
For want of my children's
Hearth and home,
Your Industry must yield!"

And crash he did at factory doors,
And broke the machinery,
And rich men cursed,
And poor men cheered,
While Ned made History!

While Ned made History, my lads,
While Ned made History!

WORLD CUP

His face was blotched, and incredulous.
"You didn't have time for the game?
You turned your back on your country,
Or your telly, which counts for the same?"

I hadn't the patience to tell him
That my country had stopped being mine,
When the wreckers had bought their explosives
From a lady in Seventy Nine.

My country was a place people made things
Out of timber and fibre and steel,
A car by Morris or Triumph,
Or Austin, with its crest on the wheel.

And English Electric provided the power
If you went for a trip on the train,
While the Health Service called for the matron
When that twinge had turned into pain.

The Coal Board was owned by the lot of us,
Our engineers kept the world in their wake,
And the sign "Made in Birmingham" told you
That what you'd just bought wouldn't break.

Yes, I did see the World Cup that one time,
When Bobby Moore held the trophy in trust,
For the union of peoples who called this place home,
'Til the idea was ground into dust

By a claque of implacable entrepreneurs
Whose yardstick was cash in the fist,
Whose country was a place you just happened to be,
And society didn't exist.

…. and now here's four songs from my play FIVE SURVIVE. The music was written by my old friend Phil Stevenson, so if you want to hear them, you'd better ask him….

THE URBAN DEVELOPMENT CORPORATION BLUES

There's a shadow in black on the river bank,
In the city that knows my name,
With teeth and claws and a hard hat smile,
He's playing the property game.

They're punching steel in the side of the hill,
Ain't no place left to hide,
I wouldn't know his face if you showed me the man
Who's taking me for a ride.

Got the URBAN DEVELOPMENT CORPORATION BLUES,
The talk's about money, and I've lost the right to choose,
She said "Things'll be fine,
Here's a friend of mine,
Taking the time to design
Your city,
Got the URBAN DEVELOPMENT CORPORATION BLUES

There's a mile of suits in the tall hotel,
You can hear the faces crack,
And the smiles are wide as contracts,
And the knives fit in the back.

And the helicopters sing in tune,
While the limos dance in line,
Around the hill where progress lives,
The place I once called mine.

Got the URBAN DEVELOPMENT CORPORATION BLUES.

LOVE ON WINDMILL HILL

In the warm of a winter's evening
We were talking, you and I,
Of rainbows at the end of a mortgage,
And ribbons of stars in the sky.
From an upstairs bay,
Through the sawn-off day
We counted the lights on the hill,
At the edge of your smile
I caught my breath, while
I knew that our time was still…

Love on, love on Windmill Hill,
Love on, love on Windmill Hill.

On the swings of a summer's morning,
We were laughing, you and I,
At the tumbling rain by the railway,
And the faces floating by.
From the home of your eyes,
And forgotten goodbyes,
We tasted the green of the hill,
Then the sun through the trees,
And the soft city breeze,
Whispered that our time was still….

Love on, love on Windmill Hill,
Love on, love on Windmill Hill.

STRUT THE MAGGIE

If you feel the night's are drawing in on England's world renown,
If foreign suns seem brighter than your own pale, wintry dawn,
Just whack on to the dance floor, and whip in glorious June,
Let's strut the Maggie, let's call the tune.

Let's strut the Maggie, let's spring the trap,
A scarlet wodge again will be emblazoned on the map,
And we'll tango in the twilight by an irridescent moon,
Let's strut the Maggie, let's call the tune.

Let's storm our saviour's message to the far flung heathen drone,
Let's wear white suits and fleece him of all he's called his own,
And let's waltz on dark verandahs while the lilting crickets spoon,
Let's strut the Maggie, let's call the tune.

Let's strut the Maggie, let's bless our race,
Let's roll our trousers up and nudge the profits into space,
And dance the unicorn blue polka while the lion stalks the coon,
Let's strut the Maggie, let's call the tune.

TURBO DEAN

In the morning light, a river of steel,
Sweatin' into town, drummin' at the wheel.
Out of the sun comes TURBO DEAN,
Screamin' gears, he's style, he's mean.
He's on the edge, Hey, Hey, Hey, TURBO DEAN,
Zap that gap! War Machine!

His time is now, there's a Honda stuck
A wide ten feet from a laundry truck.
A flash of fire, and Dean hits base,
He's three yards closer, a guy with face.
He's on the edge, Hey, Hey, Hey! TURBO DEAN.
In control! Dream Machine!

Still overtakin', Still only makin'
SMOKE.
Still overtakin', Still only makin'
SMOKE.

There's a poundin' fist on the iron trail,
Dean is trapped in the belly of the whale.
But TURBO grit will beat that jam,
He's got seven thousand R - P - M!
He's on the edge, Hey, Hey, Hey. TURBO DEAN.
Load that dice! Speed Machine!

The beast is loose, the foot goes down,
A rebel yell is comin' into town,
Through the steamin' Hell of the right hand lane
Comes screamin' DEAN, MOTOR MAN!
He's on the edge, Hey, Hey, Hey, TURBO DEAN.
Watch that grease! Suicide scene!

Still overtakin', Still only makin'
SMOKE.
Still overtakin', Still only makin'
SMOKE.

At Heaven's gate stands a quiet guy,
The race is run, the tank is dry.
A rubber scar marks a life that's cold
Of a man the road just couldn't hold.
He's on a cloud, Hey, Hey, Hey, TURBO DEAN.
Drive that sky. Through eternity.

….. and these are two poems from my play GETTING THE STORY BACK. Set in 1916, they are my attempt to write in the character of a country parish priest, caught between his love for his surroundings, and the war which rages a little way beyond his world….

LINES SPOKEN TO A SOLDIER
On his return to the front

No evening words can hold you,
And yet you turn to touch my face,
Spring mist across the weald recalls
The whisper of your wild embrace.

If what we lent the other spans
The hollow of the days to come,
Then that same love will shame the rage you run to
And your blunt beauty hush the mustering drum.

Walking Alone

Walking alone, at the lank end of Autumn,
Under the solemn fleet
Of swallows, Egypt bent
In the sun's withered stare,
I saw a badger, shining and alert,
Tracing his fallow kingdom.
I followed, down the hawthorned track,
Above the scented cutting.

Once, skirting the willow beds, he turned,
And held me with my father's eyes;
I sank beneath the question,
Hugging the damp earth.

At the far edge of the wood, we came
To a long abandoned house;
Nettles crowded its slant stone,
And ivy rooted among its flanks.
A shadow flared, and my companion
Was received, I knew not how,
Into that unrighteous green.
I drove on, parting nature's rude imperium,
And pitting my goatish strength
Beyond the mottled door.

On the stained landing,
Silent as a school room, I faced my prey.
Nailed to a high beam, in a glass-fronted case,
The badger crouched, cramped in fear
At the point of death. I wrenched the coffin
From the wall, and hurled it into the stairwell,
Following its echoed destruction
In a fall of splintered light.

At the foot of the stairs he lay.
I knelt beside him. There was blood at his mouth,
And he was smooth, and warm.

The sun was down. The swallows gone.
The scent dry at the coming of the ice.
I sat at the lip of the cutting,
Where the steam had lately flowed.

….. and finally, back to education, in whose delightful, passionate and infuriating bosom I have laboured these past seventeen years. I dedicate this poem, and this slim volume, to all those teachers who have the guts to want to improve our children, and to all those children who have to face them on wet Monday mornings….

TODAY'S LESSON IS HISTORY

At the end of a war in which
Many of the combatants themselves
Had found the confidence to dream
Of a new, classless society,
R. A. Butler's 1944 Education Act
Ironically strode a three-tier social landscape,
In which the Public Schools
(Themselves enjoying a labyrinthine hierarchy)
And the lesser private institutions
Prepared their isolated inhabitants,
Whether they desired it or not,
For a life of board-room decision
In post-war Administration, both Home and Colonial,
The law, the Secret Service and the Church,
The armed forces, the BBC, medicine,
Education itself, financial institutions, Industry,
And the media, though it wasn't called that then.
Oh, and The Arts. They were also expected to promote
Comforting images of distinction, such as riding to hounds,
The society pages in elite magazines, the London "season,"
Grouse, pheasant, stag and otter shooting, trout fishing
On private estates, and occasional philanthropy.

The Grammar Schools, with carefully screened access to
The less glamorous universities,
Were to provide a mezzanine establishment
Of accountants, GPs, estate agents, state school teachers,
Factory, bank, cinema, railway and bus station,
Labour Exchange, Local Government,
And department store managers.
Positions of rank in the Police Force

Were also considered appropriate.
Technical Schools for Boys were to produce
Draughtsmen, designers of industrial spare parts,
And architects of smaller public buildings,
Roads, and housing estates, mainly Council.
High Schools for girls were intended to supply
Housewives for the more confident suburbs,
Nursing Sisters, nannies, librarians, and women
Who could look respectable getting off buses.
Ex-pupils from all three were to be relied on
To show restraint in saloon bars after church on Sundays,
And engage in debate on the irresponsibility of the young,
And the lasting benefits of home ownership.

The Secondary Modern Schools, for all State-Educated
Children who failed the Eleven-Plus examination,
Were to prepare reasonably articulate operatives
For the complex machines of factory shop floors,
Shop assistants, garage mechanics, bricklayers,
Plumbers, plasterers, road menders, waitresses,
Butchers, bookmakers, painters and decorators,
Sometimes self-employed, so long as they kept their noses clean,
Council estate housewives gossiping in parks,
While their children smeared cheap sweets
Over hand-me-down cardigans,
The local Bobby, farm labourers, footballers, tobacconists,
Pub landlords, bus, train and taxi drivers, hospital porters,
Postmen, bus conductors, ticket collectors, cleaners,
Ladies maids, milk, laundry and bread roundsmen,
Tradesmen, who had their own entrance in those days,
Carpenters, other-ranks, and cinema projectionists.
They were also expected to contribute amusing displays of
Social vulgarity at football matches, in "palais" type dance halls,
And outside pubs, after closing time on a Friday night.

The 1945 Labour government, enjoying an unprecedented
Majority, and with a programme of social support,
"From the cradle to the grave" and the nationalisation
Of key industries, saw no reason to challenge these divisions,
Even though many of the new policies found their inspiration
In R. H. Tawney's angry identification of the Public Schools
And the Monarchy as the two great barriers to social progress.

When a nation weary of rationing returned the Tories to power
In 1951, the new government saw no benefit in abandoning
The National Health Service, Social Security, British Railways,
British Steel and The National Coal Board. Indeed, these
Core institutions, paid for from the public purse, would become
The engines of an industrial awakening which would enable
Britons to take seriously the phrase "You've never had it so good."

Education, as was only fitting, was left untouched.

It was not until the practical premiership of Harold Wilson,
Which began with Labour's return to power in 1964,
That a genuine and coherent challenge to social inequality
Was presented to a nation intrigued by the possibilities
Made available to them through television's
"Window on the world", a cinema and theatre
Turning its back on "Springtime in Mayfair," and playfully,
Angrily, joining the search, in newspapers, books, music
And magazines, art school, photography, and local politics
For the men and women who lived cheek by jowl
With billowing factories, loving and dying
In rooms you wouldn't see in Country Life,
But who also had cause to investigate philosophy,
To contribute as equals in the shaping of the nation's future,
Even to become writers and artists and thinkers themselves,
And maybe get to number one in America.

The Labour Party in the mid nineteen sixties,
To the discomfort of Conservative opinion,
Which now appeared to nod at the edge
Of a moth-eaten world in which the soiled flags of scandal
Hung limply over clubs for former gentlemen,
Voted to spend more money on State Education
Than on weapons, an explosive insolence in itself,
But worse was to follow. As the new policy unfolded,
It became clear that Labour meant what they'd said
On the doorstep, at election time.
They were going to build a new kind of school.
A school in which each and every child in the country
From whatever background, would be valued equally,
And allowed to develop their particular abilities,
Whatever they might be, "at their own pace."

It was called the Comprehensive School.

Labour was pragmatic. There was a feeling in the Party
That to vote the Public Schools out of existence would lead
To unpleasantness, and possibly violence in remote shires,
So they opted instead for a system of State Education
Which would guarantee achievement through, on the one hand,
A fierce commitment to literacy, mathematics and science,
And on the other a working day which recognised the value
Of Sport, the arts and activity as motivating and enjoyable.
Add that to small classes, nice chairs and highly trained teachers,
The support of the new Polytechnics and the Open University,
A building programme which plonked glass architecture slap bang
In the middle of every community, wherever it happened to find
Itself, then you had the beginnings of a social revolution based,
Not on barricades, but on belonging, opportunity and involvement.

And by golly it worked.

Alongside insistent representatives of ourselves, like
Albert Finney, Tom Courteney and Rita Tushingham,
Celebrating the regional agonies of life in the cinema,
And the impudent power of a Lennon/McCartney song,
We started to notice, as the sixties became the seventies,
How the plum had fled the accent in university lecture halls,
On the six o'clock news, railway station announcements,
In office and factory boardrooms, in theatres, art galleries,
Even in pulpits, though not with out the odd ecumenical scuffle,
Television advertisements for washing machines and cigarettes,
Discussion programmes and the Wednesday Play on the BBC,
And how being considered important brought responsibility,
And an invitation to confront our own prejudices.

The trouble was, even the big five Public Schools were losing cash.

Dependent on the bank accounts of the middle classes
For the propping up of a Britain that knew its place,
And appalled at the way in which large numbers of them
Dropped their kids off at the gates of the new schools,
They moaned, muttered, quoted G.K. Chesterton,
Harrangued, button-holed, bought whole rounds,
Intrigued, conspired, schemed, plotted, connived,
In smoke-filled rooms in St James's and Whitehall,
And cloistered enclosures at the edge of battlegrounds
Where the war was to be fought. To the last breath,
If necessary, for social division as a hereditary right.

In the end they found a champion whose lonely fears of equality
Were as wretched as their own, and whose taste for regulation
Echoed in the dark corners of a discomforted psychology.

The government of Margaret Thatcher, elected on a tide
Of simmering industrial discontent, and racial anxiety,
And determined to replace an economy based on production
With one enjoying the fruits of commodity finance alone,
Recognised, in 1979, that an education system designed to liberate
The human spirit could not be tolerated in a country
Where the movement of money from pocket to institution
Was to be the only yardstick
By which personal happiness could be quantified.

The 1988 Education Reform Act has no precedent
In its destructive rage. No Puritan zealot
Ordered the closure of hope with such authority.
The National Curriculum, numbering, packaging, testing,
Defying the humanity of sport, enjoyment, reflection,
Debate, putting on a show, or just sitting on the grass
Having a chat with people who know that only effort
Is required on the journey to achievement, was the paper
On which the sentence was handed down, and, because
They thought a few voices might smudge the print,
And because enforced school poverty was central to the policy,
The government cobbled together a legion
Of mountebanks, dupes, fakes, hypocrites, witch finders,
Villains, stooges, buffoons, sneaks, swindlers, Pharisees,
Snivelers, Quislings, shysters, liars and fourflushers,
And called them, with some wit, it has to be said,
The Office for Standards in Education,
And sent this oozing pus on the wound of politics
Out into the learning environment, with strict instructions
To blame teachers for the dismal outcome of the act,
And to terrorise them into silence.

Which is what teachers were supposed to do with their pupils
In the good old days.
But when they started wearing corduroy jackets,
And encouraging a critical view of the world,
And when Teddy Boys, Punks, Mods, Rockers and Skinheads,
(Whose function was to intimidate the population
Into voting for an authoritarian government)
Started reading books, passing exams, and having opinions,
And joining hands in protest against racial discrimination,
War, nuclear power, nurses pay and pit closures,
Then hammer and anvil had to meet,
And submission to the future grind insisted upon.

Blair's New Labour Party splattered contempt
On the destitute morality of Tory education policy,
And promised change with seething indignation.
But when they came to power, in 1997, they forgot
The price of betrayal, and plumped for more of the same,
Dancing, with their former antagonists,
In the ashes of the Comprehensive dream.

Logic persuaded them. What is the point of enlightening children
They said, if all they'll have to do as adults is say "enter the pin,"
Or "remove the card," or else have a go at managing the script,
If they're up for a bit of promotion?

And so it goes back. Tom Courteney has been replaced
By Hugh Grant, no relation, though he does have the knack
When it comes to light comedy.
The members of Oxford's Bullingdon club, on the other hand,
As unfunny and brutish a collection
Of Public School pranksters
As you will find in the dingy annals of power,

Have achieved that very thing, while New Labour's "Academies"
Have been described as "the new grammar schools"
By someone calling himself "Lord Adonis,"
Who obviously thinks that the whole thing is pretty much sewn up,
Making his call for the "private sector" to share their "DNA"
A responsible and philanthropic determination that the leftovers
From charity banquets will be equally distributed amongst the
Deserving poor, now that the old order has been restored.

Or perhaps it hasn't.

After thirty years of sustained assault by politicians
And their bridled hacks in newspapers and on the telly,
And shackled to a management culture trained to target
Independent thought wherever it breaks from cover,
Teachers in ex-comprehensives still walk with purpose into work,
Still demand of their students that they recognise
Their uniqueness, and, sometimes grumpily, suggest
That their achievements, won at the very front of their being,
Will have a practical and lasting meaning. Still run the disco,
Still excavate cash from the tombs of pockets, and forfeit days
On trips to Alton Towers and the museums of Barcelona,
Still provoke interest behind the mask of the national curriculum,
Ref the match, sing in the choir at Christmas, build sets for plays,
Still drive the bus, put on art shows, lab nights, music concerts,
Experience patience when talking to parents, write references,
Look attentive at year meetings, pretend to understand
Power Point presentations at in-service days, pick up litter,
Find lost dinner money, joke with the tea lady, pull fights apart,
Lend their guitars and precious books, tidy their cupboards,
And get A Level results as good as you'll find anywhere.
Pack all that with a spirit of community, a touch of vivacity,
And a refusal to desert the future, and we may yet complete
The journey, knowing that the ruts in the road on the way
Have been peppered with seeds of hope.